The Book of Luck

Published in 2024 by Hardie Grant Books (London)

Hardie Grant Books (London)
5th & 6th Floors
52–54 Southwark Street
London SE1 1UN

hardiegrantbooks.com

British Library Cataloguing-in-Publication Data.
A catalogue record for this book is available from the British Library.

Book of Luck
ISBN: 9781784887698

10 9 8 7 6 5 4 3 2 1

Publishing Director: Kajal Mistry
Senior Project Editor: Chelsea Edwards
Design: Double Slice Studio
(Amelia Leuzzi + Bonnie Eichelberger)
Proofreader: Clare Double
Senior Production Controller: Sabeena Atchia

Colour reproduction by p2d
Printed in China by RR Donnelley Asia
Printing Solution Limited

The Book of Luck

Luna Knight

Hardie Grant

BOOKS

Contents

Introduction

'I believe luck is preparation meeting opportunity. If you hadn't been prepared when the opportunity came along, you wouldn't have been "lucky".'

Oprah Winfrey [1]

From ancient symbols dating back millennia to social media trends for inviting luck into your life, the concept of luck has fascinated and divided people in equal measure for centuries. Some believe ardently in superstition, refusing to fly on Friday the thirteenth, crossing the road to avoid a black cat and considering their whole day ruined if they step under a ladder, while others dismiss such attitudes as nonsense, insisting there is no such thing as 'good' or 'bad' luck. Whatever your beliefs, there is no denying that some things in the universe seem to be entirely out of our control, down to chance. And given that these things can have a huge impact on our lives, it seems only natural to want to understand the idea of luck a little better.

LUCKY PEOPLE

We might think of good or bad luck as being something small, like hitting a run of green lights on the way to work or having one of 'those' days when every little thing goes wrong (you spill your coffee, lock yourself out of your car, find yourself stuck in the lift with your really tedious colleague whose emails you've been ignoring) but there are some people in history for whom luck – or a lack of it – seems to take a much more significant form.

Consider Violet Jessop, a stewardess and nurse originally from Argentina. In September 1911, she was working on the RMS *Olympic* when the boat collided with another ship. Luckily, the *Olympic* made it back to port, and about six months later, Jessop transferred to work on another ship – the *Titanic*. She survived the *Titanic*'s tragic sinking, during which about two-thirds of the passengers and crew died. Four years later, during World War One, Jessop was working as a nurse on board the RMS *Britannic* when it was sunk by a German naval mine. Again, she survived. She is often described as one of the luckiest people in history, given that she survived three significant marine incidents, but some would disagree and argue that it's somewhat unlucky to find yourself caught up in so many dangerous situations.

Another famous example of luck in action is the story of the discovery of penicillin, one of the most significant scientific and medical developments in history. Alexander Fleming discovered this game-changing antibiotic when he returned from a holiday to discover that one of the Petri dishes in his laboratory had become contaminated and was growing mould. When he looked at it under the microscope, he found that this mould had inhibited the growth of the bacteria he had originally been studying. This accidental discovery went on to revolutionise the future of medicine.

CAN WE MAKE OUR OWN LUCK?

So, is it all down to fate, or are there steps we can take to bring ourselves luck?

You may have seen the trend for 'Lucky Girl Syndrome', which swept social media in 2022 and 2023. This trend was similar in concept to the idea of manifestation, and at the time of writing, #luckygirlsyndrome had 1.6 billion views on TikTok. Those who shared the idea claimed that they had dramatically improved their own luck by adopting the attitude and mantras of a lucky person, telling themselves things like, 'I am so lucky, things always work out for me.' The idea is similar to those behind the Law of Attraction and the Law of Assumption: that adopting a positive and abundant attitude and 'acting as if' will attract these things to you. Could telling yourself that you are lucky actually make you luckier?

If this all feels a little far-fetched, let's look at something with a more scientific approach. Richard Wiseman, psychologist and author of *The Luck Factor*, spent over a decade studying luck and interviewing more than a thousand volunteers who considered themselves 'lucky' or 'unlucky'. His findings are fascinating – and encouraging. He found that 'lucky' people tend to have a more positive attitude towards life: they are likely to expect things to work out well for them, and are open to opportunities and new experiences. 'Unlucky' people, meanwhile, tend to expect the worst, avoiding new experiences and often not even spotting opportunities. In one experiment, Wiseman and his researchers placed a five-pound note on the pavement outside a coffee shop they knew two of their volunteers would be visiting. The volunteer who considered herself 'unlucky' stepped right over it, while the 'lucky' volunteer spotted it at once. Could it be that part of luck is as simple as being open and paying attention?

Wiseman certainly thinks so, explaining: 'Luck [is] not a magical ability or a gift from the gods. Instead, it [is] a state of mind: a way of thinking and behaving. People are not born lucky or unlucky, but create much of their own good and bad luck through their thoughts, feelings and actions.'[2] He explains that 'lucky' people are more likely to persevere when times are tough because they have positive hopes for a good outcome, while 'unlucky' people are more likely to give up, or not even try in the first place. This can often reinforce their opinions of themselves as 'unlucky' – after all, you can't get the job if you don't even apply, just like you can't win the lottery if you don't buy a ticket.

LUCKY CHARMS: BELIEFS AND SYMBOLS

Whatever your beliefs about the existence of luck, it's an idea that transcends borders and cultures – just about every society in history has had good-luck symbols and practices to ward off bad luck, from hanging horseshoes over doorways to throwing salt over one's left shoulder. In this book, we've gathered a collection of more than fifty good-luck symbols, charms and rituals from all over the world, and shared some of the stories and beliefs behind them. Even if these symbols aren't magical guarantees of good luck, they can focus your energy and remind you to adopt a positive, proactive, 'lucky' mindset. And if it does turn out that they have mystical powers, then that's a win-win. We've also shared a series of exercises, rituals and practices you can adopt to help make luck a bigger part of your own life.

CHAPTER 1

Numbers

11:11

Numerology is the belief in the mystical meaning of particular numbers. In numerology, an 'angel number' is a short sequence of repeating numbers, like 333 or 22. The number 1111 (or 11:11) is thought to be a particularly potent example. The number 1 symbolises unity and creativity, and this is enhanced by repetition. If you glance at the clock and see that the time is 11:11, it's a sign of alignment and support from the universe. It suggests that you're on the right track and that the universe has your back. It can also be a good time to make a wish.

For many people, the date 11 November (11/11) holds particular significance, as the end of World War One was announced at 11am on 11 November 1918 (Armistice Day). So even if numerology doesn't appeal to you, this number can still be seen as a symbol of peace and hope.

The number 7 is probably the most popular lucky number in the Western world, with so many people choosing it as their best-loved digit that a 2014 online survey named it the world's favourite number,[3] while a 1976 study found that it's the most likely number to be chosen if we're asked to pick a number between 1 and 10.[4] So what is it about this number that holds so much magic for us?

There's no doubt that the number 7 finds its way into our lives and popular culture over and over again. There are seven days in the week, seven colours in the rainbow, seven continents, and seven wonders of the world. The seventh son of a seventh son is thought to have magical powers, while every bingo caller will announce this ball with a cry of 'Lucky number 7!' And we all know how fond *Friends* character Monica Geller is of this particular number ...

8

Many people are instinctively drawn to the number 8 because of its pleasing symmetry and similarity to the symbol for infinity (∞), but this number is considered particularly lucky in China, where it is associated with prosperity and wealth. The word for number 8 (bā) sounds similar to the word meaning to generate wealth (fā), and the number is so highly regarded in this culture that number plates or house numbers that feature it can change hands for significant sums of money.

In 2008, the Summer Olympics were held in Beijing, and the opening ceremony was carefully scheduled to start at the auspicious time of eight minutes past eight, on 8 August: 8.08pm, 8/08/08.

9

The number 9 is associated with luck and positivity in a number of cultures across the world. In Thailand, it is considered lucky because its pronunciation is similar to that of the phrase 'moving forward', meaning it is associated with progress and opportunity. In China, meanwhile, the number 9 symbolises eternity, which is why you might receive a bunch of 9 – or even 99! – red roses from your lover on Valentine's Day. The incredible Forbidden City in Beijing, once home to Chinese emperors, is said to have 999 buildings containing 9,999.5 rooms. Given that it's been standing since the 1400s, it looks like all those 9s are paying off.

Get Lucky

How to invite your lucky number into your life

Whether you're a devotee of the number 7, a fan of the number 9 or a maverick who chooses your own lucky number (see page 17 if you need some help with this!), finding ways to bring your lucky number into your life can help you to attract luck and notice opportunities.

If your lucky number is on the larger side, you can use the principles of numerology to reduce it down to a more manageable digit that still holds all the power and meaning of the original. For example, if your lucky number is 689, then you can do the following:

$6 + 8 + 9 = 23$
$2 + 3 = 5$

This means that in situations where your lucky number is too big to invoke in its standard form, you can use the figure of 5 in its place. (Note: if you get to the number 11, there is no need to turn this into 1 + 1 = 2, as 11 is considered very lucky, and it's generally a pretty manageable figure, too!)

CHARM BRACELET

Buy a charm bracelet or necklace, then attach your lucky number of charms to it. If you like, you can double down on the luck by selecting charms that are associated with good fortune – the rest of this book will give you plenty of inspiration on that front. Wear the bracelet or necklace often, particularly on days when you feel you really need the universe to be on your side. Another option, if charms aren't really your thing, is to weave a bracelet using your lucky number of threads, and wear that instead.

COIN POUCH

Fill a small coin pouch with your lucky number's worth of coins and carry it in your pocket or purse. Coins are already lucky symbols (see page 106) associated with wealth and success, so this is a great way to keep your lucky number with you.

DRAW IT ON

Sometimes the simplest things can be the most effective. Just take a pen and write your lucky number on your skin. This simple technique is a favourite of pop star Taylor Swift, who has explained she writes her lucky number (which is, rather unusually, 13) on her hand before shows.[5] If you really want to commit, perhaps you could even consider a tattoo!

COUNTING COMPLIMENTS

If you're having a day when luck just doesn't seem to be on your side, try to generate some positivity by putting good energy out into the world. Think of your lucky number and reach out to that number of people, either in person, by phone, by letter, by email or by text. Send each person a compliment, letting them know something you value about them. You'll give them a boost, and you'll feel better too, for having engaged in a positive activity. Grounding this action in your lucky number will enhance these feelings and help turn your day around.

MARK THE MOMENT

Look out for your lucky number on the calendar and the clock. Try and take a moment at that time, or on that day of the month, to really focus on the number and enjoy its energy. Find ways to bring the number into your life using the time and dates. If your lucky number is 6, for example, perhaps you'll set your morning alarm for 6.06am. If your lucky number is 3, why not arrange to take the day off on 3 March (3/03) and do something just for yourself? As you get used to looking out for your number, you might even find you naturally glance at the clock at just the right time to see it pop up.

PAY ATTENTION

As we learned in the introduction, so much of luck is about paying attention and being open to opportunities. Looking out for your lucky number is a great way to practise this. The more you do it, the more you'll find your number pops up. Perhaps it'll be the number of the bus you catch, the time of your train or your room number at a hotel. Whenever you see your number, take a moment to notice and appreciate it, letting that feeling of luck flow into your day.

How to choose a lucky number

If you don't feel like you have a lucky number that really speaks to you, then follow the guidance above about paying attention, but this time look out for any numbers that seem to pop up for you again and again. Do you keep seeing the same number in addresses and bank statements, or on number plates? Do you find yourself glancing at the clock at the same time each day?

Alternatively, the next time something good happens to you, pay attention to any numbers that might be connected with it, however loosely. Did you get an email offering you a new job at 10am? Did you perform particularly well during a sports event when your competitor number was 27? Perhaps you had a really great first date when seated at table number 6? Start to pay attention to this number and see where else it comes up for you.

CHAPTER 2

Crystals & Colours

Jade

In traditional Chinese culture, jade was often worn by nobility and was considered a symbol of authority, power and longevity. It was also often placed in tombs, as it was believed to preserve the soul of the deceased, helping them achieve immortality, with some royalty of the Han dynasty even buried in full jade body suits.[6] It also has sacred significance in some ancient Mesoamerican cultures, where it was used for ornamentation and in burial rites.

This beautiful, ethereal stone comes in a range of colours, but the best known is probably green jade (see page 25 for more on luck and the colour green). Jade is associated with peace, tranquillity and friendship, as well as prosperity and abundance, so it's easy to see why this calming, grounding stone is so closely associated with luck. In recent years, jade has also become extremely popular in the world of skincare, with people using jade facial rollers or gua sha tools.

Tiger's Eye

This beautiful, dark-coloured stone is known for the flash of golden-red that shoots through its middle. Like its namesake the tiger, this stone is associated with courage and strength, and is often believed to have protective properties. It is traditionally worn to ward off negativity and guard against the evil eye, and Roman soldiers were even said to wear it in battle for protection.

The tiger's eye is thought to have a grounding energy that promotes clarity and bravery, and is linked to good fortune and focus, which makes it a great stone to use if you really want to nail a performance or presentation. Go get 'em, tiger.

Red

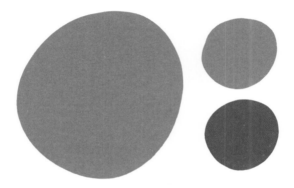

Red is famously seen as a lucky colour in China, where it is worn at weddings and celebrations for Lunar New Year. Legend has it that the New Year used to be blighted by the appearance of a fearsome monster called Nian, until the people discovered that Nian was terrified of the colour red – and loud noises. Now, in China, New Year is marked with hundreds of red lanterns, which festoon homes and streets, while firecrackers are lit to make sure Nian stays well away. Children are also given gifts of red envelopes containing money. Red is now so well associated with joy and prosperity that in Chinese stock exchanges, stocks that are rising in value are highlighted in red – a colour that usually shows a fall in value in the West.

Green

Instantly evoking nature and abundance, the calming hue of green is associated with luck and positivity in cultures all over the world. In Ireland, it's linked to the lucky four-leafed clover (page 38) and the mischievous leprechaun, while in the Middle East it is revered as a sacred colour of Islam, associated with paradise. In China, green is linked with the powerful stone jade (page 20) and thought to symbolise wealth and fertility.

Some people feel less positively about this shade, associating it with the 'green-eyed monster' of jealousy, but with its links to spring, new growth and revitalised landscapes, for most of us, green is well worth welcoming into your life.

Yellow

Summoning up thoughts of sunshine and warmth, yellow can bring an upbeat boost to your day, adding a splash of colour and positivity. In Thailand, yellow is the royal colour, and it is considered particularly lucky to wear it on a Monday. In China, too, it is associated with royalty and power, and there is even a mythical Chinese sovereign known as the Yellow Emperor.

In some South American countries, it's considered good luck to wear a brand-new pair of yellow underpants on New Year's Eve, to welcome luck, prosperity and positivity into your life for the year ahead!

Orange

This vibrant, joyful shade oozes positivity and energy. Orange is considered a sacred colour in India and is associated with the precious spice saffron. It is said to symbolise Agni, the Hindu god of fire, so the colour often features heavily in religious celebrations.

Mandarin oranges are traditionally given, shared and eaten at Chinese New Year, seen as a symbol of good fortune and calling in happiness and prosperity for the months ahead.

Get Lucky

Creating a vision board to attract luck

Many people use vision boards to help them manifest their desires or focus on their goals. This is a similar idea, but here we will be creating a vision board that is all about drawing luck into your life.

As with a regular vision board, you can use a tool like Pinterest to make a digital board if you prefer, but sitting down with pens, paper, magazines and glue is always going to be a great way of fully engaging with this task.

Spend some time gathering words, items and images that
say 'luck' to you. You can cut out words from the pages of
magazines or write them down yourself. Some luck-filled words
to include could be:

serendipity

windfall

good fortune

coincidence

opportunity

kismet

delight

For images, choose pictures that resonate with you and seem
to suggest luck or good fortune. This might include symbols
and items from this book, or images that evoke feelings of
wellbeing, such as sunshine, people laughing, or accidental
moments of symmetry.

Arrange your chosen words and images on a large piece
of paper or cardboard and, when you're happy, glue them
in place.

Try to spend a few minutes every day looking at your vision
board. It will help you to become more aware of opportunities
for luck in your everyday life, and give you the sense that luck
is part of your world.

CHAPTER 3

Plants

Heather

Heather, especially white heather, is associated with luck, and was a favourite flower of Queen Victoria. The links between heather and good fortune have their roots in Scottish folklore. The Scottish poet James Macpherson wrote about the Celtic bard Ossian and his daughter, Malvina. Malvina's fiancé, Oscar, was killed in battle, and a messenger brought her the sad news, along with a spray of purple heather Oscar had picked as he lay dying. As Malvina wept over the heather, her tears turned the flowers white, and she made a wish that all those who found white heather in future would be brought good fortune, bestowing happiness on others even in the midst of her grief.

These days, sprigs of white heather are often found in bridal bouquets, symbolising good luck for the happy couple.

Acorn

Oak trees live for hundreds of years, and can take 20-50 years to become mature enough to bear fruit. It can be strange to look at a tiny acorn and imagine it has the potential to grow into a huge tree that could live for centuries. Acorns were traditionally carried by soldiers and travellers for health and protection, and are closely associated with strength, longevity and power. They are particularly symbolic in Norse mythology, as the oak tree is linked to the mighty god of thunder, Thor, thanks to the tree's ability to weather huge storms. Some people believed that placing an acorn on their windowsill could protect their home from lightning. The acorn can be seen as a powerful symbol of potential, reminding us that even small things can be full of promise and possibility.

Lucky Bamboo

Also known as 'curly bamboo', *Dracaena sanderiana* is not technically a bamboo plant, but it has long been associated with luck, wellbeing and prosperity. It's often used in feng shui to promote the flow of luck and harmony into the home. Lucky bamboo is known for its distinctive curly stalks, the number of which is said to have an impact on the type of luck that the plant will bring the owner: for example, two stalks will bring luck in love and relationships, while five stalks promise good health.

These appealing little plants are popular housewarming or New Year's gifts, but it's important that you care for them properly or your luck could run out.

Four-leafed Clover

How many of us spent happy summer days as kids searching for four-leafed clovers in the garden? These botanical wonders are exceedingly rare – one study found that the chances of finding a four-leafed clover are 1 in 5,076.[7] It is probably their rarity that explains why they are considered lucky; after all, if you're lucky enough to find one, it's a good sign that luck is present and active in your life. Although they are particularly associated with Ireland, four-leafed clovers are worn as a symbol of luck and prosperity all over the world. Some people believe they can be carried as protection against negative forces, while others think they give the holder the power to see fairies. Another popular belief is that giving a four-leafed clover to someone else can double your luck – after all, sharing is caring.

Fairy Tree

In Ireland, *sceach*, fairy trees or fairy bushes, are considered sacred places for the *sídhe*, or little folk, and are said to mark the gateways between our world and the fairy world. They are usually ash or hawthorn trees, and can often be found standing alone in the middle of a field, sometimes surrounded by a protective ring of rocks or stones. Damaging these trees is considered to be very bad luck, and farmers will go to great lengths to avoid harming them when ploughing their fields or harvesting their crops. In 1999, a planned motorway bypass in County Clare was reworked to avoid damaging a fairy bush after a local folklorist warned officials that moving it or cutting it down would bring bad luck – and could even increase the risk of fatalities when the road was completed.[8]

Get Lucky

Daily affirmations

You may already be familiar with the practice of reciting daily affirmations as a way to attract the energy you want into your life. If you want to invite more luck into your orbit, it makes sense to focus your affirmations around this.

Spend some time thinking about what you want your affirmation or affirmations to be. Here are some ideas to get you started:

I welcome luck into my life.

I am happy, I am healthy,
I am lucky, I am loved.

I make my own luck.

I am a lucky person.
Things always go my way.

I trust my luck.

You'll notice that these affirmations make use of the present tense. Wording your affirmation as if it's something you already have rather than something you want makes it more powerful; that's why we say 'I am lucky' rather than 'I want to be lucky'.

When you've chosen your affirmation, write it down on a piece of paper. Use a pen in a colour that you associate with luck (see pages 24–27 for ideas). Stick your affirmation somewhere you will see it every day. A popular option is to stick it on the frame of your mirror, so you'll see it in the morning when you get ready. Some people like to stick their affirmations to the sides of their computer monitor or on the inside of the front door so they see it each time they leave the house. Every day, repeat the affirmation to yourself aloud, focusing your energy on making it come true.

Making this part of your daily ritual will help you become more open to luck and more aware of opportunities as you move through your day.

CHAPTER 4

Animals

Swallow

In Portuguese culture, swallows are seen as a symbol of love, loyalty and hope, and people often decorate their homes with clay swallow figurines. It's considered a great honour if swallows make a nest on your property, because these beautiful birds are known for returning to the same nest year after year. Thanks to their loyalty, swallows are often associated with fidelity, so they frequently feature in wedding decorations, and in ancient Greece they were associated with Aphrodite, the goddess of love. Because they are migratory, the first sighting of a swallow is considered lucky, as it's a sign that spring is on the way.

Sailors often have swallow tattoos to symbolise travelling long distances and returning home again; traditionally, they would get a swallow tattooed on one hand to mark 5,000 miles travelled, and another on the other hand to mark 10,000 miles.

Albatross

We may be quick to associate the albatross with bad luck thanks to the phrase 'the albatross around my neck', but that's all down to Samuel Taylor Coleridge's famous poem *The Rime of the Ancient Mariner*, in which a sailor shoots an albatross with his crossbow, bringing disaster to his ship. While it is considered incredibly bad luck to kill an albatross, sighting one is a sign of good luck for sailors. With their vast wingspans and ability to cover great distances, albatrosses were once considered somewhat supernatural, and were believed to carry the souls of dead mariners – so if you spotted one flying over your ship, it was a sign that a deceased sailor's spirit was guiding you and ensuring your safe passage.

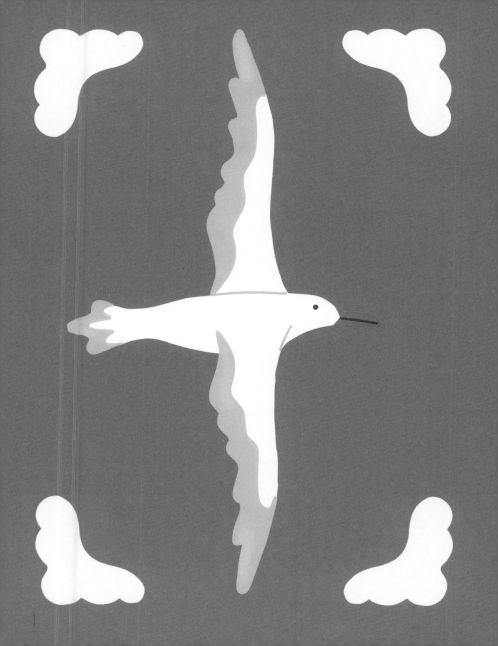

Goldfish

With their vibrant, shiny scales, goldfish can look like little jewels swimming along, so it's no surprise to hear that they're associated with luck and prosperity. In China, they are a popular symbol of good fortune, and even feature in feng shui, as their beautiful colour and soothing movements resonate calm and encourage the flow of luck into your home. They have similar associations with harmony and good fortune in Japan.

In 17th-century Europe, it was considered good luck for a man to present his wife with a gift of goldfish on their first wedding anniversary, although this practice died out somewhat when goldfish became more widely available.

Tortoiseshell Cat

Although cats – especially black cats – are sometimes considered unlucky because of their association with witches, the tortoiseshell cat is generally seen in a more favourable light. This isn't a distinct breed, but is instead a cat with very particular pretty markings in black and a lighter colour, often a reddish brown or golden shade. In Ireland, tortoiseshell cats are believed to bring good luck to their owners, while in the US, they are associated with wealth – so much so that they are sometimes called 'money cats'. In Japan, fishermen used to believe that taking a tortoiseshell cat on their boats would protect them against shipwrecks and ghosts. Just one in three thousand tortoiseshell cats is male, meaning these little guys are considered luckier still due to their rarity. However, some folkloric beliefs suggest that a strange tortoiseshell cat walking into your home is a sign of misfortune, so if you're going to spend time with one, make sure you're acquainted first.

Magpie

We tend to associate these striking black-and-white birds with bad luck, thanks to the nursery rhyme – 'One for sorrow' – but if you go on to read the rest of the rhyme, there are some very positive connotations to be found with multiple magpies:

One for sorrow

Two for joy

Three for a girl

Four for a boy

Five for silver

Six for gold

Seven for a secret, never to be told.

The reason that a solo magpie is considered unlucky is thought to be because the birds are known for mating for life. If you see one on its own, it's a sign that its mate has died, and so a lone magpie can be considered a symbol of death. However, if you do spot a singular magpie, all is not lost; any bad luck can be swiftly counteracted by saluting the magpie (or tipping your hat, if you're wearing one) and extending a friendly greeting, such as, 'Good morning, Mr Magpie.'

In China, conversely, a single magpie is a symbol of good luck, while in South Korea, a lone magpie is thought to be a messenger bringing good news, or a sign that welcome visitors are on the way.

Get Lucky

Keeping a luck journal

You're probably familiar with the idea of a gratitude journal,
where you take some time each day to write down three things
for which you are grateful. A luck journal is the same thing,
with a slight difference – you're writing down three things
that have made you feel lucky that day. They may often be
the same things you would write down in a gratitude journal
– the things that make us feel grateful also tend to make us
feel lucky – but there is also space here to really focus in on
those little moments of serendipity when luck has shown up
for you throughout your day. Perhaps you got on to a crowded
train carriage and happened to spot a friend you've been
wanting to catch up with; maybe the roads were unusually
clear of traffic and you got home way faster than usual. Take
a moment to record and remember these little sparks of luck
throughout your day. Just as practising gratitude helps us
welcome more positivity into our lives, so actively recognising
and acknowledging luck helps us notice new opportunities and
keep ourselves open to more happy coincidences. Plus, if you
ever have a day when you feel like nothing is going your way, it
can be really reassuring to look through your luck journal and
remind yourself that hey, you're a pretty lucky person.

Pig

Pigs are associated with good luck, prosperity and happiness all over the world. They're often linked with wealth, which is why we kept our pocket money in piggy banks as kids, and the fact that pigs are relatively cheap to feed and can reproduce quickly meant they were traditionally associated with plenty.

In Germany, gifts of marzipan pigs – *Glücksschwein* – are exchanged at New Year for good luck, while in Norway, the phrase *'Heldiggriss'* is often uttered to express that someone has had good fortune. It literally means 'lucky pig', but it's not considered an insult – it's a very positive thing to say, acknowledging the brilliant luck that the person in question has enjoyed.

These clever creatures also have a place as one of the twelve animals of the Chinese zodiac, representing good fortune, wealth, peace and patience.

Elephant

Elephants are believed to symbolise luck, power and wisdom. In India and South-east Asia, they are revered and often feature in religious iconography: for example, Ganesha, the Hindu god of wisdom, new beginnings and luck, is depicted as having the head of an elephant, while the deity Indra, king of the gods, is seen riding a white elephant named Airavata. Elephant statues are often found in homes as symbols of protection, and (particularly in Western countries) it is thought to signify abundance if their trunks are pointing upwards.

Although in the UK, the term 'white elephant' is often used to describe something expensive to maintain and difficult to get rid of, in Thailand, white elephants are associated with luck and royalty as they were once kept by the royal family. These regal creatures remain the country's national symbol to this day.

Frog

We've all heard the fairy tale about the princess kissing a frog to turn it into a prince, but have you ever considered that it might be luckier just to keep the frog? Frogs are associated with abundance, wellbeing and good fortune, and can also be seen as a symbol of transformation, thanks to the almost-magical change they go through as they develop from tadpoles into frogs.

In Australia, the Aboriginal people consider frogs a sign of good luck as they are generally found by water, so the sighting of a frog is a good indication that water is near, or perhaps that much-needed rain is on the way. Similar beliefs are found in some Native American cultures, where the frog's association with water also means it is linked with the idea of cleansing and renewal.

In Japan, many people keep an origami frog in their wallets. The Japanese word for frog, *kaeru*, has another meaning: 'to return'. So keeping a little paper frog in your wallet ensures that any money you spend jumps right back! In China, the *Jin Chan* – money frog – statuette is a symbol of, you guessed it, wealth (see page 118), while the ancient Romans and Greeks associated these hoppy little guys with luck and fertility.

Ladybird

Ladybirds (or ladybugs in the US) are said to get their name – and their association with good luck – from the story that French farmers prayed to the Virgin Mary for help when aphids started destroying their crops. The Blessed Lady responded by sending them these little bugs, who happily devoured the aphids and saved the harvest. Farmers still associate ladybirds with good luck (and healthy crops) today. French folklore even credits the ladybird with preventing a wrongful execution; it's said that a ladybird kept landing on the condemned man's neck, and the executioner didn't want to swing the axe and kill the innocent insect, so the execution was delayed – and soon after, the true culprit was caught.

Ladybirds often have seven spots (see page 12 for why this is such a lucky number), and it's said that if one lands on you, you should count its spots. Depending on which version of the belief you prefer, the number of spots either indicates how many years of good luck await you, how many children you will have, or how many months you have to wait until your greatest wish comes true.

Get Lucky

Lucky rituals

Many people have specific lucky rituals that they stick to religiously when they are hoping for a positive outcome at an important event. For example, the great composer Tchaikovsky liked to take a two-hour walk every day, and believed that if this walk was a minute longer or shorter, his composing wouldn't go well that day. Olympic champion Mo Farah always shaved his head before races, while tennis ace Serena Williams always wore the same pair of socks for her matches. This doesn't mean that Mo Farah had a magic razor or that Serena Williams had a pair of socks with mystical powers. What's important is the ritual of shaving, putting on the socks, going for that walk. Doing this is taking a moment to focus on positive energy and get into the right headspace for whatever challenge you are about to face.

Think about your own habits and try to identify one that you can turn into a good-luck ritual by focusing on it as you get ready. Alternatively, you can create a new one. It might help to think of a situation you've been in recently when things have really gone your way, and look at what you did when you were getting ready that day – is there something you can replicate? Perhaps you'll decide that the act of putting on a particular shade of lipstick is going to be your lucky ritual; maybe you'll listen to a certain song or use a particular pen. The important thing here is that you're taking a moment to focus on what you want to achieve; the lucky item or ritual is just an anchor for the positive energy you're bringing to your day.

CHAPTER 5

In the Sky

Moon

With its silvery light and changing appearance, it's no surprise that the moon has captivated us for centuries, with different cultures attaching varying myths and meanings to its waxing and waning.

A new moon, or the very first sliver as the moon begins to wax, is considered a good time to start a business or propose marriage, and it's a particularly lucky time to move in to a new house. It's also thought to be lucky to 'show' a new baby to a new moon, as the growing moon will bless the baby with its potential. However, it's bad luck to view the new moon through a window, so make sure you're looking directly at it.

The full moon signifies abundance, and is a popular time to practise manifestation rituals. However, it has also traditionally been associated with madness – and werewolves!

About every two and a half years, we have what is known as a blue moon, when an 'extra' thirteenth full moon occurs during one 12-month period. This is because the lunar calendar is slightly different to our calendar year. Its relative rarity is where we get the phrase 'once in a blue moon', and it's considered a particularly lucky full moon. It's said that if you pick flowers by the light of a blue moon, you'll be blessed with abundance in the coming month.

Another special moon-based event is a lunar eclipse, which tends to happen about once every six months. In Tibetan folklore, it's said that any good deeds carried out during a lunar eclipse are multiplied.

Rainbow

In the Bible, a rainbow appears in the sky at the end of the Flood as a promise that the destruction it brought would never be repeated, and the rainbow is now seen as a symbol of hope and new beginnings. In Irish folklore, it's believed that if you follow a rainbow to its end, you'll find a pot of gold – but be warned, it's likely to be guarded by a leprechaun, and they can be rather tricksy. Another common belief is that you should make a wish when you see a rainbow.

Despite the rainbow's beauty and many positive connotations, it's not all good news. Researchers have found that in an amazing 124 countries across the world, including Sumatra, Australia and Brazil, it's considered bad luck to point at a rainbow,[9] with a traditional belief in Hungary that pointing at a rainbow would cause your finger to wither.

North Star

For millennia, travellers in the northern hemisphere have used the North Star as a guiding light to help them navigate and find their way. The North Star sits almost exactly above the North Pole, making it a valuable tool for working out which way is north. It is particularly associated with sailors, who used it to find their way at sea, and the North Star is a recurring feature in traditional sailor tattoos.

The North Star is considered lucky because once you have spotted it, you will always be able to work out which way to go. In a world that can be chaotic and full of change, the North Star represents purpose, focus and constancy.

'But I am constant as the northern star of whose true-fixed and resting quality there is no fellow in the firmament.'

William Shakespeare, *Julius Caesar*

Shooting Star

If the North Star is valued for its constancy, shooting stars are considered lucky for just the opposite reason – they're fleeting, fast and hard to spot, so if you see one darting across the night sky, you can count yourself very lucky. Growing up, many of us were taught to wish upon a shooting star, and it's a common practice the world over. Some people think this can be traced back as far as ancient Greece; the philosopher Ptolemy explained that shooting stars were caused by gods pushing them out of the way as they peered down on us from the heavens, so making a wish when you saw one made good sense, as the gods were likely to be listening. However, other stories from Greek myths say that shooting stars are actually stones thrown by Zeus when he is angry.

Sixth-century Chinese philosopher Confucius suggested that shooting stars are departed souls making their way to the afterlife. This belief is seen in many other cultures, and can be a source of great comfort. Whether you think they're souls, stones or something else, there's no doubt that the sight of a shooting star always feels like something special.

Get Lucky

Inviting luck in

Of course, we could just sit around and wait for luck to happen to us, but as we've been learning, a big part of being a lucky person is being open to luck. Here are some ideas for how you can invite luck in to your life.

OPENING UP YOUR SPACE

If things are feeling a little static and stagnant in your life and you're ready for some change, try to kick-start change by re-energising your space. Open all the windows, invite in a fresh breeze, and let your home fill with new energy. Imagine that you're doing the same thing for your life – opening up where you may have been closed off, and allowing new opportunities to flow in.

TRY SOMETHING DIFFERENT

Part of being open to new opportunities is trying new things – despite what the rom-coms tell us, you're unlikely to stumble upon the love of your life in your local supermarket, and doing the same things day in, day out doesn't create much space for luck to do its best work. Experiment with making small changes to your usual routine. Get off the bus a few stops early and walk through the park; try going to a different coffee shop or grocery store; pick up a book by an author you've never read before. These small changes might seem insignificant, but they can lead to a wider shift within you, and signal to the universe that you're ready for new possibilities.

LOOK THE PART

To remind yourself to remain open to luck (and perhaps to attract it to you), try adding some lucky symbols to your day-to-day life. Perhaps you'll dress in a certain colour associated with luck (see pages 24–27); perhaps you'll hang a horseshoe over your door (see page 104). Maybe you'll pick and wear a lucky charm (see pages 112–113) or get a tattoo of a goldfish (see page 50). Whatever you choose, use it as a way to make luck a part of your life.

CHAPTER 6

Food

Eggs

Eggs have long been associated with fertility and new beginnings, and they play an important part in Easter celebrations all over the world, whether they're emptied and painted in bright colours or the chocolate variety.

In the UK and the US, cracking open a double-yolked egg is thought to be particularly lucky, as it contains twice the treasure and is seen as a signal of abundance. Some people even believe that eating one can bring on a marriage proposal!

If you're not lucky enough to come across a double-yolked egg, you can challenge a friend to a game of egg tapping (sometimes known as egg 'jarping' in England). Each player takes a hard-boiled egg and the pointed ends are tapped together. The winner – the person whose egg doesn't break – will enjoy good luck. Variations of this game are played all over the world, including in England, Croatia, Bulgaria, Greece and Assam in India.

Carp

In Poland, it's traditional to prepare a big feast to eat on Christmas Eve, with 12 dishes to bring the diners good luck in the coming 12 months. The centrepiece is a carp, and it's considered lucky for each diner to remove a few carp scales and keep them somewhere safe for the next year. Most people keep them in their wallets, where they are thought to attract money.

In the Czech Republic, there is a slight variation on this tradition; diners take a few carp scales and place them underneath their plates for the duration of the meal. When they've finished eating, they transfer the scales to their wallets for safe keeping.

Grapes

If you celebrate New Year's Eve in Spain, you may be surprised to see people gobbling grapes as the clock strikes midnight. This tradition is known as *Las doces uvas de la suerte* ('the twelve grapes of luck'), and the idea is to eat one grape for each strike of the clock to ensure good luck and happiness for the year ahead. The practice became popular in the early 1900s, and is still eagerly observed today. Some people enjoy their grapes at home with family, while others gather in town squares and other public places to ring in the new year together and share the tradition.

The custom is also popular in Latin America, although there are some variations. For example, in Peru it's believed that if you eat your 12 grapes while sitting under a table, you can attract luck into your love life.

Soba Noodles

Another foodie tradition associated with New Year's Eve is the Japanese custom of eating 'New Year's noodles' – toshikoshi soba. The long, thin shape of these buckwheat noodles is thought to signify a long and happy life, while the fact that they are easy to bite through symbolises breaking away from the old year and starting anew. It's definitely a delicious way to celebrate a fresh start.

Pomegranates

With their dozens of shining, jewel-like seeds, it's no surprise that pomegranates are associated with prosperity, fertility and luck. In Greek mythology, these beautiful fruits are famously linked to Persephone, who ate six pomegranate seeds while in Hades, and so became destined to spend six months of each year there as Queen of the Underworld, and six months on earth among the living.

In Greece today, many people take part in the unusual tradition of smashing a pomegranate on New Year's Day for good luck. Usually, the pomegranate is smashed open on the front door of the house, and the idea is that the number of seeds that burst out signify how much joy and good fortune its residents will enjoy in the coming year. Some people take the pomegranate to church with them first so that they'll be doubly blessed.

Herring

In Poland, Scandinavia and Germany, it's common to eat pickled herring on New Year's Eve for good luck, usually at midnight. The fish's silvery colour is thought to attract wealth, while the fact that they are plentiful is a sign of abundance for the year ahead. As people from these countries made their way to the US, the tradition is also practised there, with people buying jars of salted or pickled herring ready to mark the new year and bring luck into their lives.

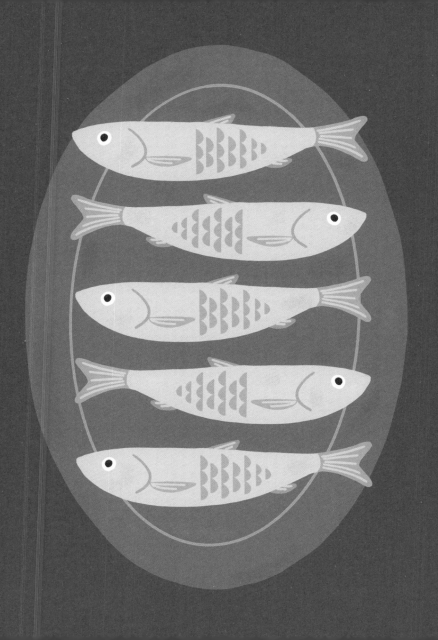

Get Lucky

Meditation to welcome luck

This simple meditation can help you to become more open to luck, putting a positive and open energy out into the universe to attract the same thing back.

You'll need to set aside 10–15 minutes, and it's best if you can do this in a calm, quiet place where you won't be disturbed. Make sure you're warm and comfortable; if you wish, you can keep a blanket close by to make sure you stay nice and cosy.

Read through the visualisation below before you start, as you'll be doing the meditation with your eyes closed. If you prefer, you can record yourself reading it aloud, then play the recording as you meditate.

If you like, you can light a candle or some incense to set the mood, then sit on a cushion with your back straight and your legs crossed, or, if you prefer, sit in a chair with your feet on the ground. If neither of these are possible, you can do this lying down or in whatever position is most comfortable for you – just try not to fall asleep!

Once you're comfortable, close your eyes and allow your breathing to become slow and steady. For a few moments, just focus on your breath – in and out, in and out.

When you're ready, visualise yourself waking up in the morning, fizzing with energy and excitement for the day ahead. Think about your favourite weather, whether that's dazzling sunshine or comforting soft rain, then picture yourself pulling back the curtains to see it.

Now picture yourself moving through your day, but at every moment where luck could come into play, visualise the best possible outcome. Your bus arrives as soon as you reach the bus stop; you get a seat on the train; you see your boss in the coffee area and get the chance to tell them about the new project you've been working on – and they think it sounds great. You walk out at lunchtime with a spring in your step, and bump into one of your favourite people; perhaps you see that the florist near your office has a half-price offer on your favourite type of flower. A table in a great café becomes available just as you approach, queues fade away, and it feels like everything you do is being supported and celebrated by the universe.

Focus on how good it feels to enjoy and appreciate those little moments and tiny wins, and notice the way they add up to create a feeling of high energy and joy.

Try to hold on to that feeling, wrapping it up inside you so you can carry it with you. When you're ready, open your eyes and blow out the candle, then step into your day with the energy of someone who already knows they're lucky as hell.

CHAPTER 7

Trinkets & Items

Wishbone

The wishbone or furcula is a forked bone found in birds, and has long been associated with superstitious beliefs. The ancient Etruscans, who lived in Italy before the founding of the Roman Empire, believed that birds had the ability to tell the future, and after a chicken died, they would keep the bones and dry them out in the sun to use in fortune-telling. The furcula was considered particularly lucky, and it was said that if you made a wish while rubbing it, your wish would come true. The Romans adopted this belief, but took to breaking the wishbone in two, and gradually the idea came about that whoever got the larger half would get their wish. The practice made its way to Britain (where wishbones were known as 'merrythoughts'), and from there the Pilgrims brought it to what would become the US, where they continued the tradition with turkeys. Today, breaking the wishbone is a customary part of the Thanksgiving feast.

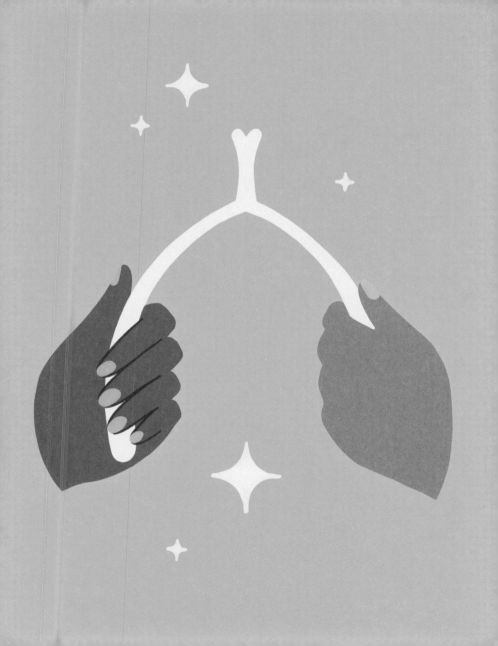

Rabbit's Foot

This rather gruesome trinket is found in cultures all over the world. Some historians believe it may come from the 16th- and 17th-century tradition of cutting off the left hand of a hanged criminal and pickling it – this practice, known as the 'Hand of Glory', was thought to bring good luck. It may have even earlier roots, as Roman philosopher Pliny the Elder is said to have claimed that carrying the foot of a hare could cure you of gout. Rabbits were also associated with witches, either as their familiars (a supernatural helper or companion, often taking the form of an animal) or as the form they might take when shapeshifting, so it's possible this connection is why the rabbit's foot charm is thought to have so much power. They became popular to carry as amulets in the 19th and early 20th centuries. These days if you come across a rabbit's foot charm, it's likely to be synthetic.

Daruma Doll

In Japanese culture, a Daruma doll is a hollow, round doll with a weighted bottom. It is thought to represent the Bodhidharma, a Buddhist monk who is said to have sat in meditation for nine years without moving, staying motionless for so long that his arms and legs fell off. The doll's rounded shape and weighted base mean that it rocks back to an upright position when it is tilted or pushed, suggesting perseverance and the ability to get back up when knocked down. Some Daruma dolls are sold with blank eyes; the idea is that the receiver paints on one of the eyes when setting a goal, and paints on the other when that goal has been achieved.

Horseshoe

Horseshoes are often hung over the doors of houses as a sign of good luck, and have traditionally been gifted to brides on their wedding day to hang over the threshold of their new home. The association of the horseshoe with luck goes back to the story of St Dunstan, who was Archbishop of Canterbury in the 10th century. Legend has it that the Devil came to Dunstan and asked him to re-shoe his cloven hooves. Dunstan took a horseshoe and attached it to the Devil's hoof with a red-hot nail, causing the beast so much pain that he begged to be freed. Dunstan agreed, but only if the Devil promised never to enter a home over which a horseshoe was hung. (Other versions of this story simply say that the whole experience just put the Devil off horseshoes so much that he swore never to go near one again.)

People disagree over the orientation of the horseshoe; some think it should be hung upright, so that all the luck stays contained, while others argue it should be hung upside down, so the luck pours out over all those who walk beneath it. Whichever way you hang it, it's also interesting to note that horseshoes usually have holes for seven nails – see page 12 for more on this auspicious number.

Coins

SIXPENCE

This British coin was first minted in 1551, and left circulation in 1980. It was worth half a shilling, one fortieth of a pound (there were 20 shillings in a pound). Starting in the Victorian era, it became common practice to stir a sixpence into the Christmas pudding batter – whoever found the coin in their piece of pudding would have good luck for the year ahead (and perhaps a dentist's bill, if they weren't careful!). Another popular tradition was to slip a sixpence into the bride's shoe before the wedding for good luck, and people still practise this today, or find a way to incorporate a sixpence into their outfit or bouquets. Members of the Royal Air Force (RAF) also used to sew a sixpence into their uniforms to bring them good luck.

LUCKY PENNY

'See a penny, pick it up, and all day long, you'll have good luck.' The idea that finding a penny is lucky is popular in the UK, Ireland and the US, with some people believing you should only pick up the coin if it is lying heads up. An Irish half-penny (a coin that left circulation in 1987) is considered particularly lucky. In Ireland, some folk tales claim that pennies are often left out by pixies, fairies or leprechauns to bring good luck to the finder. It was also traditional to give the buyer some of their money back at a market 'for luck' – often just a penny.

Nazar/Evil Eye Amulet

Have you ever heard the phrase 'If looks could kill?' We all know what it's like to be on the receiving end of a withering glare, and the 'evil eye' is a curse believed to be caused by someone aiming a malicious stare in your direction. It's particularly associated with envy or wishing harm on someone. Belief in the evil eye is found the world over and dates back centuries – references to it can be found in the works of ancient philosophers including Plato and Pliny the Elder.

There are various charms thought to protect against the evil eye, but this one is probably the most famous. Found in countries including Turkey, Greece and Iran, this amulet is usually made of blue glass and has the appearance of an eye. It's believed to be lucky to carry one with you or to hang it over the door to your home to protect you from the evil eye, and perhaps even direct the cruel gaze and bad wishes back at the person who cast them.

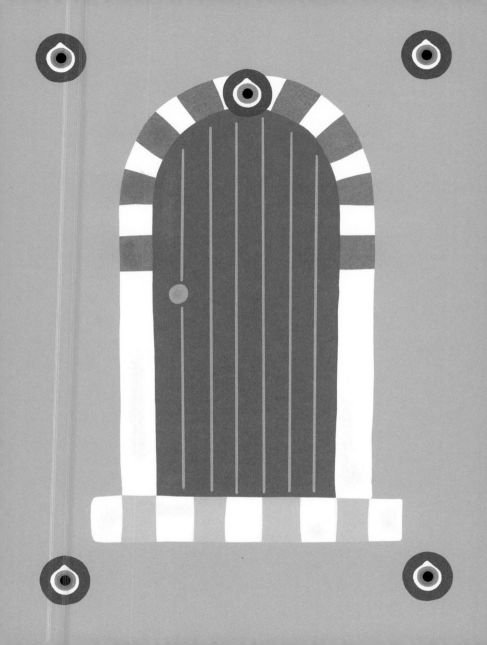

Maneki-neko

These adorable little cat figurines originate in Japan, and they're often found near the entrances to homes or businesses. They may look as if they are cheerfully waving, but *maneki-neko* actually means 'beckoning cat'; they sit there, beckoning with their paws, welcoming visitors and inviting in good fortune. There are various stories about the *maneki-neko*'s origin, including one about a travelling samurai who was beckoned into a temple by a cat. Just as he got inside, a heavy storm broke out – luckily, he was already safely indoors and able to take shelter.

These cat figurines are often depicted holding a coin or a fish in their non-beckoning paw – both signs of abundance.

Get Lucky

Choosing a good-luck charm

Many people have a good-luck charm they like to carry with them to bring them good fortune and confidence throughout their day. These might be traditional 'lucky' items like those discussed in this book, but sometimes they are seemingly random objects that hold great meaning for that particular person. They can be innocuous items, like the champagne cork Ernest Hemingway used to carry in his pocket, or a little on the unusual side, like the pouch of baby teeth (her own!) that model Heidi Klum has claimed to keep about her person. Former US president Barack Obama is said to keep a collection of small items and trinkets given to him by well-wishers; each morning, he selects one or several of these items and places it in his pocket as a lucky charm imbued with the giver's good wishes. Opera singer Luciano Pavarotti always used to pick up a bent nail from backstage before performing, and was so committed to this habit that stage hands were said to leave a few lying around to make sure he could always find one with ease.

A lot of people already have a good-luck charm without even realising it; it might be a necklace they always wear, a key ring they've had for years, or a particular tie they like to wear for important interviews. Sometimes, we only realise these items are important to us if they go missing. So take some time to look at the items you regularly interact with, and see whether any of them 'speak' to you as a lucky charm. Or, if something particularly lucky happens to you one day, pick an item that you happened to have with you, such as a coin or a bracelet, and adopt it as your own personal good-luck talisman.

Dala Horse

These pretty carved wooden horses, usually painted red and decorated with striking patterns, have become a national symbol of Sweden, and are often given as gifts on important occasions like weddings to bring good luck to the receiver.

The Dala or Dalecarlian horse dates back to the 17th century, but they didn't become popular worldwide until much later. At the 1939 World Fair in New York, the Swedish section featured a huge Dala horse that towered over the exhibition at an impressive three metres tall. It so delighted attendees that it sparked a trend for Dala horses in the States, and more than 20,000 were shipped to the US in the next year.

Gris-gris

A *gris-gris* is a small pouch that is often worn or carried as a good-luck amulet. They originated in West Africa, specifically Ghana, and are associated with Voodoo. These little pouches may be decorated with scripture or traditional words, or they might contain rolled-up pieces of paper marked with meaningful words and symbols. Sometimes they hold other significant objects, such as herbs, roots, stones or coins, depending on their intended purpose. The *gris-gris* is thought to be a very powerful item, and can be viewed negatively because they can also be used to create curses.

Jin Chan

The *Jin Chan* (money frog or money toad) is a Chinese symbol of good luck and wealth. These little statues are usually gold in colour, although they can also be made of other materials, including jade (see page 20). The *Jin Chan* usually has three legs and red eyes, and sits with a coin protruding from its mouth. The mythical being on which these statues are based is said to appear during a full moon near homes or businesses that are about to receive good fortune. The statues are popular in feng shui, and are thought to attract wealth and wellbeing. Some people like to boost their effectiveness by tying a piece of red ribbon around them or by placing them on a piece of red cloth or paper – but it's important they are not placed facing a door, as that could cause the wealth and luck to flow out of the home instead of into it.

Nénette and Rin Tin Tin

These string dolls became popular in Paris in 1918, at the height of the First World War. In the midst of fierce fighting, they became symbols of hope and good luck, and were carried by civilians or worn pinned to their uniforms by soldiers. The two dolls are joined together by a piece of wool or string, and it is essential that they should never be separated. It's also said that their good luck only works if they are gifted, so buying your own wouldn't work. Sometimes, they are joined on their string by a third doll, a baby called 'Petit Lardon'. A US Army Corporal serving in Europe was so taken with the little dolls that when he rescued a litter of German Shepherd puppies whose kennel had been damaged by bombing, he adopted two and named them Nanette and Rin Tin Tin, taking them back to the USA with him. Rin Tin Tin turned out to have a skill for performance, and ended up becoming a silent film star, appearing in 27 Hollywood movies.

Worry Dolls

Originating in Guatemala, worry dolls (or *muñeca quitapena*) are tiny figurines made from wire, wool and scraps of fabric. They are thought to be inspired by the myth of the Maya princess Ixmucane, upon whom the sun god bestowed the remarkable gift of being able to solve any problem. These dolls are often given to anxious children to help them with their worries. The idea is that you should whisper your worries to the dolls before going to bed at night, then sleep with them under your pillow. By morning, the dolls will have taken away your worries or shown you a solution. They have come to be seen as a symbol of protection and good luck thanks to their ability to ease anxiety and help people navigate difficult situations without getting bogged down in their worries. They say a problem shared is a problem halved, and worry dolls can serve as a valuable reminder of all you have overcome in the past.

Scarab Beetle

These beetle-shaped amulets from ancient Egypt were often placed in tombs or around the necks of mummies to help the deceased in their onward journey to the afterlife. They were modelled after dung beetles, which were associated with the sun god, Khepri, who people believed rolled the sun into the sky in the morning in the same way that the beetles roll their balls of dung. Khepri is often depicted with a scarab's head for this reason. Scarabs were associated with rebirth, regeneration and renewal. They eventually became associated with good fortune and protection, and were worn by the living as good-luck charms.

Cornish Piskie Charm

Piskies (or piskeys, or pixies) are mischievous little fairy beings found in the folklore of Cornwall, UK. Often described as wrinkled old men, they were said to help elderly or infirm travellers find their way – but if they came across younger or more able-bodied explorers, these tricksy creatures might impishly lead them astray on the wild moors. Stone circles and 'barrows' (mounds of earth, often built over graves) were thought to be favourite haunts of the piskies, leading some people to avoid such places. Despite their reputation for mischief, piskies were thought to reward people with good luck if they were allowed to live in small holes or hovels within the home, and some were even said to help out with housework. Piskie charms were often worn or displayed around the house for protection and good fortune. Sometimes they even appeared on door knockers to guard against unwanted guests and keep misfortune away from the house. Many piskie charms feature the Queen of the Piskies, known as Joan the Wad; 'wad' means 'torch', and she is often depicted as carrying a torch to guide people to safety.

Cornicello

Popular in Italy, particularly Naples, the *cornicello* or 'little horn' might look like a chilli pepper (especially as it's often red), but it's actually modelled on an animal horn, with the red colour coming from the fact that they were often traditionally made out of red coral. These horns are thought to provide protection against the evil eye (see page 108), and are often worn as charms, or hung in homes or from the rear-view mirror in cars. The use of horns as symbols of protection is thought to date back to the Neolithic period, when horns were often hung outside the home, and representations of the *cornicello* have been found in ancient cities including Pompeii. As well as protection, these horns are associated with virility, and have been linked to Priapus, a Greek fertility god.

Get Lucky

Finding the positive

As we learned in the introduction, researchers have found that 'lucky' people are more likely to persevere when times are tough, and it's possible that their apparent luckiness stems from their ability to see problems as challenges rather than feeling defeated, and their tendency to look for the positive side in a difficult situation.

There is, of course, a risk to taking this too far. Toxic positivity – the insistence on 'good vibes only' and refusal to accept or acknowledge the existence of hardship – helps no one, and sometimes things really are difficult or painful. But on a smaller and more realistic scale, a certain amount of healthy reframing can go a long way towards adjusting your attitude and helping you feel more able to tackle the challenges that life loves to throw our way.

Take some time to reflect on something difficult that you've been through in the past. Start small: there's no need to dive head-first into the most devastating thing you've ever experienced and, as we've established, not everything is going to have a silver lining. Life-changing events and painful losses are probably best explored in a safe space with a trusted friend or therapist. For this exercise, it can be useful to begin by choosing something from which you now have a certain amount of distance, such as a break-up that felt disastrous at the time, but from which you have now moved on.

Think about how painful it was back then, and then allow yourself to think about the ways in which your life has since improved. If that boy hadn't dumped you, for example, perhaps you'd never have decided to go travelling for the summer, and you'd never have met all those wonderful people and had those amazing experiences. If you hadn't been made redundant from that job, you might never have made the decision to retrain and start the new career you now love. It could be something tiny – you might have missed your stop on the bus, but it meant you discovered a brilliant new bookshop on a street you wouldn't usually have walked down, or perhaps you lost a favourite earring, but searching for it meant you ended up giving your home a much-needed spring clean. It can be as simple as acknowledging: 'That was hard, but it has made me stronger.'

Learning to recognise the potential and positives in a challenging situation doesn't mean you ignore the challenge or that it isn't painful or disruptive, but it can give you more of a sense of control and an idea of how to move forward. It can also remind you that you have survived difficult things before, so you know you can do it again. You can't always control what happens to you, but you do at least have a certain amount of control over how you respond to it. Over time, when difficulties arise, you may find that you have trained yourself to look at them slightly differently – with the mindset of a person who is lucky, even when bad luck strikes.

CHAPTER 8

Symbols

Ankh

Based on the hieroglyphic symbol for 'life', the ankh is an ancient Egyptian symbol signifying eternal life, regeneration, wisdom and healing. It's also called 'the cross of life', and sometimes 'the key of life' or 'the key of the Nile' due to its shape. It is often depicted being held by deities, and is particularly associated with Isis, the goddess of fertility, magic and healing, who is sometimes shown holding it and using it to revive the souls of the dead in the afterlife. Now it is seen as a symbol of good luck and protection, and is often worn as an amulet.

Hannun- vaakuna

Mac users will instantly recognise this symbol as the one used on the 'Command' key on their computers, but the *Hannunvaakuna*, also known as the St Hannes Cross or the St John's Cross, is actually an ancient symbol originating in northern Europe. Most widely used in Finland, it was seen as a symbol of protection and good luck, and for centuries it was traditional to paint or carve it on buildings, furniture and household items. It has also appeared on coins and in embroidery designs. These days, it's still seen as a good-luck charm, but it is also used on maps and signs to signify tourist attractions and sites of cultural importance.

Barn Star

This five-pointed star is often seen hanging or painted on barns in the US, particularly in Pennsylvania. Also known as 'primitive stars', these are associated with German-American and Dutch-American farming communities, and are believed to bring good fortune and ward off evil and bad luck. Some people believe that the colour of the barn star is particularly important, ascribing certain meanings to different shades: for example, black barn stars are for protection, while green ones are for fertility and growth.

Hamsa

This hand-shaped symbol is often worn or displayed as a mark of protection and good luck in Middle Eastern and North African countries, and its use dates back thousands of years. Also known as the Hand of Fatima or the Hand of Miriam (Fatima was the daughter of the Prophet Mohammed, while Miriam was the sister of Moses), the *hamsa* is thought to protect against the evil eye (see page 108). 'Hamsa' means five, which corresponds to the five fingers on the hand, and this revered symbol is associated with various religions, including Islam, Judaism, Hinduism and sometimes Christianity. The *hamsa* is often depicted with an eye in the middle of the palm to deflect evil gazes and negative forces. When worn or hung with the fingers pointing upright, it is thought to bring protection and ward off evil, and when the fingers are pointing downward, it is said to welcome in abundance and positivity.

Get Lucky

The luck list

This exercise is similar to the luck journal (see pages 56–57), and you might find it useful to refer to your luck journal here if you've already started keeping one. Take some time to write a list of all the times you can remember luck really being on your side, from winning a raffle or making an amazing catch in a game to unexpectedly being invited to a party and meeting your soulmate. The very act of writing a list like this is a delightful exercise in itself, as it reminds you of some brilliant experiences and can really boost your sense of yourself as a lucky person.

Now work your way through the list and try to look out for any similarities between these lucky moments. Did a lot of them happen because you broke with your usual routine that day, or attended an event you weren't originally planning to go to? Did they come about because you were paying particular attention to your surroundings – or perhaps because you had allowed yourself to relax and let your guard down after a long day? When you've found a common theme or themes, spend some time journalling about how you can make the most of this discovery. Is it a sign that good luck tends to find you when you push yourself out of your comfort zone? If so, how can you do this more often? Perhaps it's something that feels entirely arbitrary, like all these things seem to have happened on a Saturday. Look at how your behaviour, attitudes or routines might be different on this day – perhaps you're more relaxed, have more time to be flexible, or have the headspace to take a more playful approach to your day. Is there a way to bring some of this 'lucky day' attitude into the other days of your week? (Sadly, this doesn't mean you can stop going to work, but it might mean you change up your boring office clothes or plan a mid-week outing to bring a little bit of Saturday energy to your Wednesday.)

The luck list is a powerful tool for reminding yourself how lucky you really are – and for discovering the ways in which you can make yourself luckier still.

CHAPTER 9

Actions & Rituals

Knocking on wood

Knocking on wood – or sometimes touching wood – is a common practice in the UK, usually after saying something you hope will come true, but sometimes in an effort to ward off misfortune or avoid tempting fate. For example, a person might say, 'The project's going really well,' and then knock on a wooden surface. The practice is seen in other cultures, from Bosnia and Herzegovina to Brazil, with regional variations, and has been in common usage since at least the 19th century. Some researchers think that the practice comes from a Celtic belief that spirits or ghosts live in trees, so you knock on wood to get their attention; others think it refers to the wood of Jesus' cross. British folklorist Steve Roud claims it actually comes from a 19th-century children's game known as 'Tiggy Touchwood', where you were 'safe' from being tagged if you were touching a piece of wood or a tree[10].

Throwing a coin in a wishing well

In folklore and mythology, bodies of water, including rivers, pools, springs and wells, are often associated with gods, nymphs and other spirits. Perhaps because water was such a valuable resource, it became common practice to leave an offering, such as a coin or another token, and perhaps at the same time to ask the spirit or god for a wish. In Norse mythology, Odin dropped his right eye into a well known as Mímisbrunnr in exchange for wisdom and knowledge of the future. The tradition dates back centuries; Pliny the Younger describes seeing coins at the bottom of a well in the second century CE, and archaeologists have found offerings such as coins and buttons dating back to 470 CE in Conventina's Well in Northumberland, UK. Today, the practice has extended to fountains as well as wishing wells, and shows no sign of abating; one in five adults say they will throw a coin into a wishing well or fountain if they see one, and the Trevi Fountain in Rome, perhaps the most famous spot for this kind of wish, makes about €3,000 a day – more than €1 million each year – all of which goes to good causes.

Throwing salt over your shoulder

Spilling salt is said to be bad luck. This may be because it was once a very valuable commodity, but the spilling of salt has also come to be associated with Judas Iscariot, the disciple who betrayed Jesus; if you look closely at Leonardo da Vinci's 15th-century painting *The Last Supper*, you can see that Judas has knocked over the salt cellar. Whatever the origin of this superstition, you'll be pleased to hear that throwing some of the spilled salt over your left shoulder will reverse the bad luck; this is believed to be because the Devil will be loitering there, peering over your shoulder and ready to cause problems, but if you throw the salt, you will blind him.

In many cultures, salt is thought to have protective properties, and a similar practice is also seen in Mahayan Buddhism, where salt is thrown over the left shoulder after a funeral to prevent any evil spirits entering the home.

Rubbing a statue

If you ever visit Harvard University in the US, you might notice that the left foot of the statue of its namesake, John Harvard, is a different colour to the rest of it: a bright, shining gold. This isn't because it's made out of a different material, it's because rubbing the foot of the statue is thought to bring good luck, and over the years so many people have done it that the foot has become burnished and smooth. The same thing can be seen on statues all over the world: in Springfield, Illinois, it's said to be lucky to rub the nose of the bust of Abraham Lincoln; while in Budapest, Hungary, tourists and locals alike rub the knees of a statue called *The Little Princess* to bring themselves good fortune. In Florence, Italy, a statue of a boar called *Il Porcellino* can bring luck to those who place a coin in its mouth and rub its snout, and a replica statue in Sydney, Australia, has a similarly well-rubbed snout. Over many decades of rubbing, this ritual can cause some statues to break down and become damaged, so it's always worth checking first to make sure touching is still allowed.

Blowing away eyelashes

When an eyelash falls loose, many of us almost instinctively – and with great care – reach for it, place it on the back of our hand or the tip of a finger, and then blow it away while making a wish. Although the origin of the practice is unclear, some people say it is to blow away the Devil, or to prevent the eyelash falling into the hands of a witch, who might use it to cast a spell on you. Even if you're not convinced on that front, there's no point in passing up a good wishing opportunity. Note: This only works if the eyelash falls out on its own – and you probably won't get far wishing on your falsies, either!

Shaking hands with a chimney sweep

Dick Van Dyke's Cockney accent in *Mary Poppins* may not have been terribly convincing, but there's no doubt that he convinced all of us that a chimney sweep is 'as lucky can be'. It's unclear where this belief originally came from; it's said that King George II of England was rescued by a chimney sweep who stepped in and managed to calm a runaway horse pulling the royal carriage. The king was so grateful that he declared all chimney sweeps lucky and deserving of great respect. Whether this story is true or not is hard to establish, but the idea certainly stuck, and it became considered particularly lucky for a groom to shake the hand of a chimney sweep on his wedding day (and sometimes for the bride to receive a sooty kiss on the cheek). In fact, Prince Philip was seen shaking the hand of a sweep just before he married the future Queen Elizabeth II in 1947, and it's still possible to hire a chimney sweep to attend your wedding today.

If you see a chimney sweep's brush sticking out of the top of a chimney, it's time to make a wish. Meanwhile, in some Eastern European countries, if you spot a chimney sweep, it's traditional to rub one of the buttons on your coat and make a wish.

Get Lucky

Making your own luck

As we reach the end of our journey into the wonderful world of luck, let's return for a moment to the Oprah Winfrey quote we shared at the start, specifically this part: 'I believe luck is preparation meeting opportunity.'

In amongst the fascinating folk tales and superstitious symbols we have explored, we have also come to understand the idea of luck not just as an entirely random force, but – sometimes, at least – as something we can seek out, engage with, and perhaps even learn from.

As we saw in the introduction, Richard Wiseman's research into luck shows that people who describe themselves as 'lucky' tend to have a more positive attitude, expecting the best outcomes and being open to new opportunities.

So let's summarise the ways in which you can apply the lessons of luck in your own life.

PAY ATTENTION

Whether you're keeping an eye out for your lucky number, hoping to spot the first swallow of spring or searching the ground for an elusive four-leafed clover, paying attention to the world around you can help you spot opportunities and bring luck your way – remember the five-pound note experiment on page 8?

INVITE LUCK IN

Make a luck vision board, try visualising a luckier life, take the time to recite daily affirmations welcoming luck into your world: all of these things will help you to become more open to luck.

MAKE SPACE FOR LUCK

Shake up your routine, try new things and keep an open mind. Luck might be trying to find you, but that's going to be a big challenge if you're keeping yourself constantly closed off. Try meeting it halfway by being less rigid and staying open to new experiences.

APPRECIATE THE LUCK THAT COMES YOUR WAY

Keeping a daily luck journal or writing a big 'luck list' will help you notice and appreciate the many ways in which you are already lucky – and it might even help you spot a few common factors to boost your fortunes.

THINK LUCKY

Think like a lucky person and learn to reframe certain challenges as opportunities. Appreciate the ways in which something that initially feels like bad luck could in fact teach you valuable lessons or bring you good things in the long run, and endeavour to keep trying.

REMIND YOURSELF THAT LUCK IS ALREADY HERE

Using lucky rituals, charms or your lucky number will help you to stay in a lucky mindset. So whether you decide to dress from head to toe in red, throw a coin into a wishing well, get a tortoiseshell cat or start counting magpies, remember that life – and luck – are what you make of them.

GOOD LUCK!

SOURCES

[1] Winfrey, Oprah. 'Thought for today: Luck.' oprahwinfrey.com/spirit/thought-for-today-luck.

[2] Wiseman, Richard. *The Luck Factor*. Arrow Books, 2003, page 172.

[3] Bellos, Alex. 'Seven triumphs in poll to discover the world's favourite number.' *Guardian*, 8 April 2014.

[4] Kubovy, Michael and Psotka, Joseph. 'Predominance of seven and the apparent spontaneity of numerical choices.' *Journal of Experimental Psychology Human Perception & Performance* 2(2):291–294, May 1976.

[5] Vena, Jocelyn. 'Taylor Swift explains why 13 is her lucky number.' mtv.com, 7 May 2009.

[6] Shuicheng, Li. 'Eternal Glory: The origins of Eastern jade burial and its far-reaching influence.' In Renfrew, Colin, Boyd, Michael and Morley, Iain (eds), *Death Rituals, Social Order and the Archaelogy of Immortality in the Ancient World*. Cambridge University Press, 2015.

[7] 'How rare are four-leafed clovers really?', sharetheluck.com, 2016 (https://web.archive.org/web/20201205113712/http://www.sharetheluck.ch/single-post/How-rare-are-four-leafed-clovers-really).

[8] Deegan, Gordon. 'Fairy bush survives the motorway planners.' *Irish Times*, 29 May 1999.

[9] Cooperrider, Kensy. 'Even rainbows have a dark side.' www.atlasobscura.com, 16 November 2021.

[10] Roud, Steve. *The Lore of the Playground*. Cornerstone Digital, 2010.